in the bare bones house of was

in the bare bones house of was

* * *

Mara Adamitz Scrupe

2020

Copyright © 2020 by Mara Adamitz Scrupe
All rights reserved.
Printed in the United States of America

Brighthorse Books
13202 North River Drive
Omaha, NE 68112

ISBN: 978-1-944467-19-7

Brighthorse Books is a small publisher of poetry, short fiction, and novels based in Omaha, Nebraska. For information about Brighthorse Books, visit us on the web at brighthorsebooks.com. For information about the Brighthorse Book Awards, go to https://brighthorsebooks.submittable.com/submit.

Brighthorse books are distributed to the trade through Ingram Book Group and its distribution partners. For more information, go to https://ipage.ingramcontent.com/ipage/li001.jsp.

CONTENTS

I. *North to South.*
3   the weather of an old house answered/ hard times come again no
5   honing's edge
6   Flood Stage
8   Wolf Trees
11   & Other Things Besides
13   Groundhog Laws of Contiguity

II. *Entanglements.*
17   Wanderer
19   Surrender Not Peace/ *Young Man Standing beside Empty Chair with Kepi and Worn Boots, ca. 1865*
22   Histories of a Colonial Garden
23   Loving
25   Plantation as Idyll

III. *Tell. Or keep.*
29   Family Wheel No Tree
31   Matoaka
33   America freed her
35   Monuments by Nature Require Brooding
36   Sailors Creek 1865 (Reenactment)
38   the iris the peony the dogwood bloom (If War Comes to You)

IV. *Grasp. Unended.*
42   About Baltimore
44   Baptist Dance
46   O Little Town (Listen)
48   Claritas
50   Green

V. *Roughing it. Smoothing it.*
54   Prester John's Book of Stars
59   Grinding Up the Seed Corn
61   in the bare bones house of was
63   & Bless

69   Notes
71   Acknowledgments

in the bare bones house of was

At the request of Mr. Edward W Sims I have sold to W & Fontaine an old house at Bridgeport for the sum of fifteen dollars

B. P. Ballowe
June 23ᵈ 1846

I. *North to South.*

* * *

A pilgrimage. Or a campaign.

A passage. Or sojourn.

West.

Or North to South.

Calling. Or called.

Voice. Or a claim.

Choose.   Or refuse.

* * *

When the bitter, devastating war was over, both masters and slaves found themselves in a world subtly but decisively changed. The shores of the Chesapeake were now left behind by the hordes of people of all conditions who were moving or being moved westward to possess the lands.

—Rhys Isaac, *The Transformation of Virginia 1740–1790*, University of North Carolina Press

* * *

* * *

THE "I" TYPE HOUSE (1790–1829)

Some historians suggest that this building type was popular because it served as a symbol of achievement. It presents the largest possible façade for a four room house.

—Rural & Urban House Types in North America,
Pamphlet Architecture 9, New York 1982

* * *

**the weather of an old house answered/
hard times come again no**

Two-pen vernacular
river rock piers.

Slate roof.

Post & peg & plank. Plaster lathe.
Beam.
Grain-paint trim.

Makeshift.

Hard times   come again   no—
Hay & herd & hoof. Peel the wallpaper
feather flock fan. Sift.   Crack.
Backfill fireplace

Trash.   I died a squirrel in this hearth
I am its carcass.

Snakeskin marrow flake stone adze   *sharp.*

Squabble scold badmouth female
Accidie: I could be black. Or

White.

Plumb-bob chimney sparrow baby bat chatter
scrum up my arm in the dark

Dread.

One widow-in-particular's fly-crusted
sulk.   Haint-blue congestion.
Desertion.

Breadth to best crest hill site
flinty arrow point wriggle up & out

Magic!

Country lawyer slave sale farmer. Served
& servant/ clay pack preacher.

Fifty years times four
athwart this knoll.

Captive kin relations-off-record.   Sold-signed
with an X.

Plat-mark fork
stake stone

& sapling.

honing's edge

congregations   droves/ teem &
school/ bottle fly brawl & brash roll up
a newspaper hit a half dozen right on into tomorrow into
the next county/ the next century   to porridge
mash

* * *

    running cedar spiny digit evergreen runs
as you'd expect thrum-hushed as blood not regretting
        nor tiding   unrepentant   neither troubled
nor striving   becalmed like our uninvited guests
this summer's eve a century & more's harvest
calls them home in their butternuts/ girls twirl
round the sound & swish of pretty in this God-
slammed country/ poet pastors muster ragged
Appomattox to Richmond/ now crumbled emblems in glass-

    fronted cases   now old heart hole
hip & bicep lawn & bonfire & whoop & murmur
palmettos sway the fear-fringed cabins swamps &
streams & mold-clotted putti crawl the crippled
plaster just barely volunteers   — those that survive —
that is we use them too like we do each other if there's
time if hunger's not got the best of us at last we'll
waste not a one whose boughs likewise shelter us/ shoulder
us/ berms/ the outer limit/ a line   we dare not cross

* * *

strange doings   where flies ruck at windows
a honing's edge a soul's divestment/ seen
utterance/ moral story/ tallow fat lamplight
murk & slight/ retreat/ cull   & void

Flood Stage

From the roof of the house (at a 12-point pitch)
look west & upriver past the northernmost tip
of the farthest bank
just over the rise
that's the stone quarry
you can see it clear from here
a bald patch of machined earth
alongside the river built in the thirties
amid pledges of progress
scarce jobs in lean times
look east in the opposite direction:
follow the S-curve downriver
past the poured concrete bridge
beyond the bluff at Bremo
you can see the scrubber stacks from here
planted in the bed of the James:
one of seven coal-fired plants grandfathered
built when the power came/ electric light
for a heartsick South
look west again
upriver toward the mountains directly across
where the land is open & rolls an old & truly
blue ridge serves for backdrop
this land
the best the most desired land made fruitful
by abundant flood settled by Tidewater planters
whose played-out soils pressed them
to the westernmost rim of the world
these people built the very best
the lodge came first
then the fine place made
Palladian stucco over red brick
four thousand acres of the loveliest richest land

still in the same hands
gazing out & across from our place
thought beautiful in our times
hollows ravines
streams that run through all seasons
but few flat spots for hopeful farming
glance in any direction
you can see it clear from here
flanked by insecure changeable borders
hands-down
the river is the wonder
spreading leisurely up & out
over the first bank   & then the second
clearing the way for temporary settlements
reflecting ponds on low ground
this red river at flood stage carrying away trees
& tires & fences
& cows & cars & people & all
their cheerful projects   sweeping
aside everything
without asking permission.

Wolf Trees

Pick a path in a distance

    Blood Root   Tickweed   Carolina Pink

in a striated thicket-formed fence an opening tougher
than chain link.   Spot the track precise and narrow-made
    down & across an
umber slope's thick in twining trees:

    Beech   White Oak   Walnut

& the odd remaining Hickory (though blight's taken most
of these)

    Pin Cherry   Mountain Laurel   Redbud

impenetrable except for deer & a black bear
I'm certain knows I'm here.

In this clearing is a truth I need to know. That I am
    nearly nothing in this world.
Still I long for land deep insidious ochre-tinged
jungle   young men endured & perished here

Once & for a cause.
Truckers & their Jake Brakes blast by.

I am too far North & too far South
too much in the present
present-most in the past.

This land deeded away reordered piece-by-
piece in that curved slanted intelligent   hand

   carved *numbered* *platted*

a civil strut & scanting
a centuries' sorting abreast the river rapids.

I descend thrice stumbling on obdurate roots:

  Creeper *Bridal Veil* *Grape Vine*

puzzling a path to the crevice floor
on either side too steep for trade
& therefore untouched
virginal in dry stream bed's warmest light imaginable
varnished/ silvered/ washed radiant in fall floods.

Hiking to the deepest place lowest & most private spot
safe & soundless bivouac I pause reach
knees half-bent arms straight back
& fall into hardwood leaf litter's humus-y

loam working its way to soil fragrant earth—
here flat on my back wolf trees dominate
tower

unmolested unlike their namesakes vanished
no banished from this wood & recollection
long before the war of white men for dominion over
everything giants stretched limbless to forty feet
for elemental survival & in particular

  air *light* *water*

the smooth Beech round stubbled grey-white
fine form straight tumoral roots *true* each a

  grandfather *grandmother* *testament*

it's as though I'm composing through a photographer's
lens swerving an uninterrupted sweep of solid
ascent/ a hundred then two hundred feet & beyond

where treetops here in winter's recess
in tangled free-form geometry

    touch   *graze*   *& twist*

& Other Things Besides

They're never the same lounging the lane
black & gold bellied rat-swoll shrub-drape poke-
lick sun-savor bask the slate terrace crick-hid
        in the rubbish bin rusted-out washers & tires &
piles of busted tools harmless warmth
suckers coiled plumb sashay up &   *flicker*

nicknamed for local personalities radio hosts & balding
TV weathermen or just on general attitude
easy-six-footer-slide-up-rough rake-the-flue bust-out
-the-shrubbery   *slam*   into-the-driver's-side-
door you'd have thought to death but   *nope*
sidle-off-nonchalant-as-a-skunk-after-a-spray   *did I*

imagine it? sinuate muscle non-associative
behavior according to the nonplussed farm agent/ city
friends with their pretty new baby girl walk the trace directly
into big-fella-munch-one-whole-while-the-other
-unfledged-cheeps-its-cleft-shell *peep* right-quick-
from-born-to

park my butt on the brick crumble snowmelt stoop
nurse an extra-hot coffee urge me up hard
but slow *go easy don't argue* slip your arm around
back of my shoulder draw me up inside one hand in my hand
the other yellow-backed-baby-copper-head-square
-aim-spade-flung-flat-out-airborne tinny   *bang*

* * *

Reticent they are
thinly venomous   *lickety-flick*
    fork-tongue heat-seekers

           * * *

Uneducated we were
    & frightened of alien   somethings
& other   *other things*   besides

Groundhog Laws of Contiguity

Around here
we have so many stories we crumple
them up & burn them
for kindling

We loan them out to the woodchucks
tunneling under the house:
a tight-lipped bunch
they have so few of their own.

In this vicinity we call out
tidings to the whorling woods
      to grackles
evangelist posses haranguing

Limb to limb
guano-dropping lore-seeding
      random neighbors
on our rural route.

Around here we have more
rumors than an apartment house
      more anecdotes
than a coffee shop more

Paraphrase than a bank branch manager
      more promise
          than a big box store
than an outlet mall.

In this neck of the woods
we divulge recount
rehash confess episodically
incidentally   *fervidly*

Over coffeecake
in the kitchen wearing worn
      slipper's
lengths of silent sip

Around here we have church chat
licentious
as loosestrife
common as vetch.

Vigorous as periwinkle
      sad
as spurge. We have post office
gossip motley as spring

Pinks in rot-rich soil hardware store
hearsay shameless
as bloodroot. We have clothesline
calumny candid

As mayapple coy as trillium
sour as skunk cabbage
meddling as ivy irascible
as burdock wanton as

Putty-root orchids. Around here
we listen close pay attention
attend lend an ear
hearken mind & mark

Conscientiously faithfully
regardfully   *particularly*. Around here
we're accountable
as *rememberers*.

* * *

II. *Entanglements.*
Of answerability.
Of memory.
Mine. Ours.

Or somebody   dead else's.

* * *

Decr 8th — 1823

Recd of W L Fontaine the sum of three hundred dollars on account of the first payment for a tract of land sold to W. Fontaine by me as Exr of my Father the money due next May

Pr Hardin Perkins

By Hardin Perkins

Wanderer

> In 1858 one of the last North American slave ships, *Wanderer*,
> illegally delivered 409 Africans to Jekyll Island, Georgia,
> from an original cargo of 487 people.
> —*New Georgia Encyclopedia*

      texting from Rabat (four degrees
                  south of Richmond)
he says he feels he is less
           than human

he imagines himself black as himself as he
      is/ himself but ancient/ a coastal African

calculating the sea by stars in chains
      while the lighter-skinned
wash in running water & Europeans
          live in huts   thus shackled

he imagines
    there's always an inside & an

outside a pen & a point of entry but no release no
    retreat nor advance only defeat yet he

imagines/ dreams   *deliverance*
          for them while reckoning

seventy-eight the number dumped
    into the swells   supposing all those
    lives gather round him now
lead him to just *one*   un-skinned
un-muscled skeleton/ ivory bag of bones accumulated

      unidentified
                in a cave

          or stacked unnamed unconsecrated deep in
          a Georgia wood next to a red-running
creek   tallied up for him

          subtracting multiplying dividing
the possibilities

          of truth the probabilities of fiction
          time-shifting from his place now as if
it were *him* on that ship (consequent adjustments
psychic accommodations)
                as if measuring for him

an immeasurable   distance

Surrender Not Peace/ *Young Man Standing beside Empty Chair with Kepi and Worn Boots, ca. 1865*[1]

Your belly hardens. & then. Softens. Putrefies. Blood-
gilt. Shuck. Strip. Become. Discharge. Pardon.   *Pardon?*
Sunburnt. Child or woman?   Fancy. Forfeit. You ask.
Again?

Seed. Reach or languish. Decay. Forage. Trade. You. Crease-
patterned. Across. Across. Your. Your opaline brow. One who.
One. Not two. Dance in the. Empty streets. Heather high.
Hollow. Set aside.   Pile. Heap.

Bearded. *Or beardless?* Vacant. Victorian tussock-ruffed
chair. Leather boots. Kepi. Busted. You don't. You'd prefer.
Preferred. Brother. *Brothered?* No longer. Him. There.
But not. Alone.   Lone.

Carte de visite: (albumen

Silver print.) Alongside. The many. Beside. Side.
By side. Batched. Gold braided. Trenched. Tattered. Shovel
stench *limed*. Half rotted. Some eyed. Some yawed.
Some nearly.

Stripped. Shoeless. Sockless. Your rations. His. Yours.
Picked. Clean. But not. Not. An ending. Day/ time. Inconsolable.
Cast.   Standpoint. Angle. Stance. Cessate. Not tender
bellicose.

---

1. Rosenheim, Jeff L. *Photography and the American Civil War.* The Metropolitan Museum of Art, New York. Distributed by The Yale University Press. New Haven and London. 2013.

Drum scape. Spry flare. Flame roll. & mock. Flash wake.
Trifling wonder. Hare & chase. Slam burlesque. Sunk.
Bottomless stupor. Boondockery. Sham. But solemn. Gay.
Camp. Gaiety. Of. Last.   Encampment.

Enchantment. Past doom. Past drill. Past parade. Past
union. Fiddle. Patch. Filch. Meat. Mete. Chicken wrung. Some
citizen's blunt. Spark up the poplars. Lamentable.
White picket. Front porch. Yard. Cripple

Fence. Black husk. Old Crow. Margin. Drift. Glume. North
light candlelight.   Sky. Home is.   Undoing. You
always. Need. Examine. For love. For rain. Brazen. Effortless.
Endless.   Peace. Sleep.

Patter. Pour. Hope. *Hope.*   Hopeful. Utopian. Argue.
Argument. Cause. Drain. Brash. Bandage. Wrap. Sore. Bash.
Stooged: *No damn.*   Good. Edge to precipice. Forward.
Rear. Drive. Hedge.

Girdle. Wither. Petition. Lee hands Grant. His finest. Never.
Never. Tincture of. Blade. Pure romance. Upright. Strip-limbed.
Tobacco fumed. Hard. By trade. Or inclination. Fervor bond
bonded. Bent.

Bondsmen. & women too. Hood-snap. Steel blind bound.
Sojourner. Clod. Divot. Split-hoof. Maggot. Manure.
Dirge. Gorse mat. Blind. Bid. Bid them. Order. Order them.
Abide. Swallow it. Stomach it. Bide.   *Bide.*

Take it. Current. Casual. Causal. Catastrophic. *Surrender*
not   peace. Unperturbed. Wedged. Wedged in.
Below. Piddle-paddle. Row. Oar. Pull. Punt. Above you.
Like a bear climbs a Pin Cherry tree. Maul. Hot

Scat. Steam. Road. Behind. Look. Behind. Behind you.   You.
Span. Outskirt. Province. Purview. Tent. Yard. Shiver stack
bayonets. Rivulet. Bottom feeder fricassee. To the top. Eat.
Feed. Gorge. Before. Until. Grass. Weeds.

Mud ooze. Shit. Hunger. Chaff. Your belly bloats. Hardens.
Softens. Lustrate. Squab & hummock. White. Black.
Mulatto. Quadroon. Blue blood. Patrician. Lace curtain silk
stocking.   Insurgency.   Subdued.

Swell. Itch. Alive with. Knee deep   in. Bygones.
Occupation. Coercion. Military law. Race as in race war. Post.
Post-Appomattox. Post-Charleston. Post-Roanoke. Post
-gunned down. *Down* on live TV. Obscure. Church

Shooter vengeance. Plunge. Plummet. GoPro twitter
tattle automatic feed. You'll know. Know   if you're hit.
Hit. Governance by Glock. Magazines. Rounds. Justice by
alias. By social. Media. Reportage. Revenge.

Retribution. Hollow point. *You mind*. Streaming. Video
spasm. Content may. Stream to the Bay: you watch them.
You watch coupling eagles swear. Paired sailing sailed
sail high. Away. Glide. Mated. Spray scrub. Airtight

Zip-tie post-service church basement sesquicentennial
supper. Nothing squandered hot or cold. Nothing
wasted crumb or scrap. All-in. Used up. Face it. Taste
it. What is the.   Shelf life of.

Grudge. Savor it. Hold it in your mouth. Blown. Grave
blossom. O be joyful/ blown away. Will or capacity.
To fight. *Scalawag*. Sap. Sapped. Sapper/ smash. Not.
Lost. Lifeless. Not. Vanquished.   Unforgotten.

Histories of a Colonial Garden

> Then, as now, paths of gravel or marl required good and constant rolling if they were to be kept in prime condition. Philip Miller in 1759 advised that such walks should be rolled when "it rains so fast that the walk swims in water," to which he added, "the person who rolls it should wear shoes with flat heels that they may not make Holes in the Walks."
> —*Archaeology and the Colonial Gardener*, by Audrey Noel Hume, Colonial Williamsburg Archaeological Series No. 7

i.

Carrot hoe: four inches wide. Onion hoe:
three. Six-inch hoe of uncertain
     origin: turnip hoe hilling hoe
beavertail hoe fluke hoe   hoe: first time

told crank down window racket side by side
ride   I think I hear   something else
shrug shoulder free hand
    flick   he can't

mean that say *that* straight out
snarl it snicker not subtle overt no bullshit
again explicit/ aggregate/ like I'm in on it
side by side ride   toothy-gap tarpaper

shacks   he means it   *means it*
one side or the other either side of a
line: hard/ lofty/ lordly driver's side
lean/ bench seat jerk beat then as now

side by side down the line: *line* down the
middle/ Middle English: *sclave* from Old
French *esclave* from the Latin *sclavus*:
look it up a paling a picket a yoke

post holes & railings & rain so fast
earth swims in her eyes in her ears
she's water she's wreckage she's gravel
pipe stem marl sweat baby red soil

  shot   she's an iron & granite
           rolling stone leveling a path
  path   she smooths it/ flattens it she
           is it   hand-hewn raw

---

nettle pinked rouged violet-skinned
confection she's a semblance-starred
        sister
innominate: *without her own*

name
        she's ashy vellum shade &
arbor kraal-built stock pen &
settle she's a labyrinth

a stave a keep she: keen keen
keening   he: fine-mannered
strut & she: stump straint hust
        scar stamp: sold

ii.

there's smolder out the high hall tonight
the difference between them

is a lull   *to look*   *up*

she   *bends her knees habitually*
at his approach she slides her eyes

from his   *his*   *the color of sky fly*
      flight

she: draw hoe
thrust hoe

he: taunt little monkey sticky heat wave
    downpour she:
one + one =   draw   thrust

Loving

> *People'd been mixing all the time. . . . I didn't know there was any law against it.*
> —Mildred J. Loving (Loving v. Virginia, U.S. Supreme Court, 388 U.S. 1, 1967)

      & as the inclinometer's swing atmospherically
plumbs the crescent's shadow & everything
      goes silent & God's radio comes on
    with the news we are all utterly
pleased with ourselves unquietly crossing

          state lines as B & W together unhindered

but private posts tweet up the contrast
      barefaced & comfortless
interiors collide with exteriors spectra colludes
      with scrutiny & hue & tone & tint
unbalance the half-light & pretty soon somebody says
something brings the outside inside   *says something*

        about difference/ unlikeness & just as

    sailors of vast seas & continents consult astrolabes
& quadrants locate the rhumb line shortest
      constant bearing by sun moon planets & stars
    you carry in your breast pocket
the one closest to your heart   in particularity

    not in conformity   we are creatures
    of so much possible magnanimity so much disaster
grief unstrung   head-ons of chance & fate & face value
    for good or ill healing or stealing your heart

        & glister's skin of privilege
promises cheek by jowl avowal *these here are your people*
but in between sooner or later there's a plain

      letting go/ duetted mimetic minute by minute
a front-porch-graced injunction a mid-summer evening's
        inflamed abettors limn the garden path

(tang & tipple & gad & juice & odd-mottled fruits
pear & peach & purpled
                plums soft-hip the clouds straddle

the tough old Box & common moss bed down
      with rose & lavender & *and* luscious romp cavort
& butterfly & bumblebee & & bee balm flame & tiny red-
gigged birds busily tickle the tenderest)

      & soil sown in by Harmattan cast northeasterly
by the great sphere's route by Euclid's intuitive geometry
      makes straight line's appetite/ encomium:
      his arm slung over her shoulder her head
resting on his: the aggregate: various parts/ skin eyelids lashes

cuticles bunions & haunches ineffable wholly inseparable
      plus imperfectly clement hinged & complete
impossible to finesse   no barriers
      existent free of suborning

as vermiculate forms weathering/ expands
      in furnace fever
released to mingle   in waked stream

Plantation as Idyll[2]

Mantled beds aquiver out four-
light gable end windows. Attic.
Under
the eaves. Post & beam
soaked. Unyielding
unnamed resistance.
Archived.
Grit & gullet.   Lush
& lurid. Sincere deceit
we'd rather not
discuss.

Pink tinged   seas.

Bootblack up close.   &
survival. & pussy
on a pallet.
It's not just
gluttony. Salt-encrusted. Male
female. Muscle
bone & speak. Day &
again

& after.   Dawn

To dusk.
& after.
Dependencies.
Ours. Theirs.
Tethered

---

2. This poem's title borrowed from Rhy Isaac's *The Transformation of Virginia 1740–1790*, page 40.

affections. Antipathies.
Hunted drunk. Rank
bitch.
Sweat & sty. Inspection:
a toe   in the tar   this house
Seethes.

Past my meet.
Out this room.

Fast
the blue shroud
mountains.   Haven.
Rived walls.
Broken bottles.
Sweetbreads for you
to swallow.

* * *

III. *Tell.*   *Or keep.*

* * *

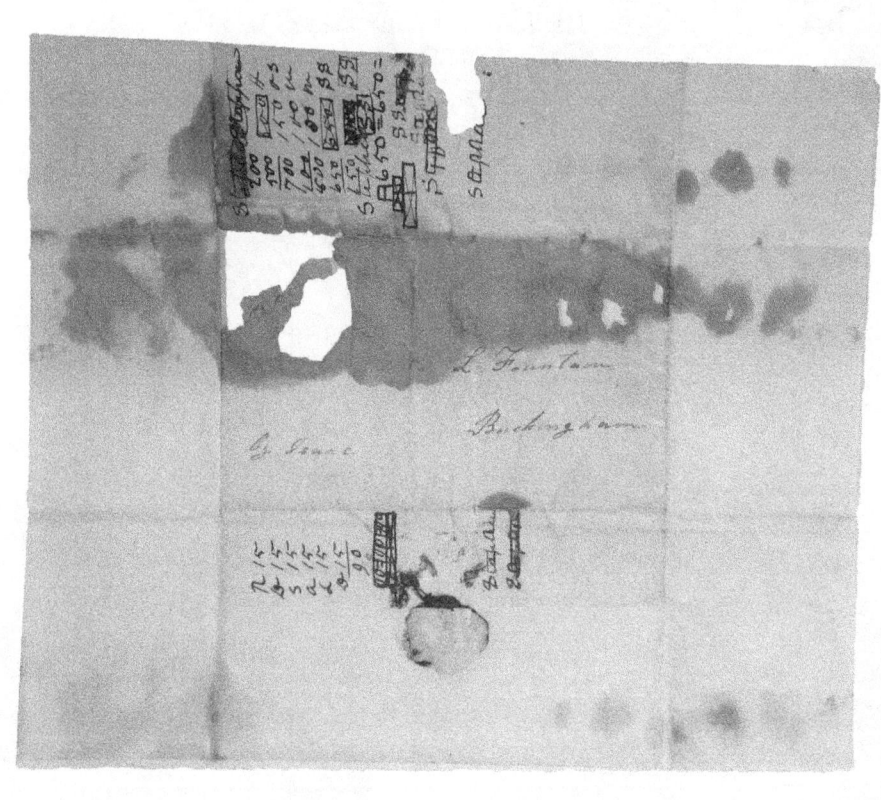

Family Wheel No Tree

Gut-caught   is a *hand*.   Brief.   But long
      enough. With a female.   Or

one after.   Corralled. Prodded.   Seize-mad.
                          Stumbled somewhere.

Or other.   Collared. At the business
      end of a.   One by.   Someplace   or.

What kind do we   —   Swung from a.
      Went on. Here. Clay stain. Corn cob. Gunny

      sack.   Down on a dirt.
Souls.   Flask.   Where the legs join the.

Bind us   blind us. Saw-tooth raw
      declension. That crop played out. Long. Long

      Long.

The money.   With it.   But not the.
      Hemmed in.   Hang on. Walk the trestle.

      The census man.   Count colors. Hides.
Hut & hovel.   Omnivorous. Taxed.

      Useless.
            Frolic.   Flail.

Fail/ rail against the. How close we how nearly. Lined
      & scrawled. Scatter-bob the rapids'.   Some

made it that way. Cabin still moonshine. Jumbled.
          Insatiate. This finest this prettiest.

This happiest. Gather.   Day.
          Reunion. No two names at the top
          of this.
Out a hub a studded.   Pegged.

No family tree. No revered.   Pair.

But.   Out.   Out   a.
          Wheel-gang.   Cluster.
          Coil. Sprawl. Sprang. Of one.
Stallion. Multiple mares. A shaft. A drudge.

          This. Appetite. A truth. Cultivate
stock. Inexorable   reap. This ligatured. This
splined   as

          as black is absorptive   as

          white is the sum   of all

Matoaka

>Matoaka, also known as "Pocahontas," was the subject of a myth in which she was said to have offered her own life for that of the European adventurer John Smith's. She later married John Rolfe, gave birth to a son, and died in March 1617 in Gravesend, England, of an unknown illness.

        she is grey wolf's Saturnine night
sickle in hand   perched on shoulders of a silvery
moon Madonna beside me

cauldron & cautery & weary representative
of various suspect alchemies
& me — atheist — I pray *I pray* to my black virgin

of Częstochowa at my Slate River landing my early bright
Blue Bunting purples flutter sun-slant safe
to forest floor   mother sister niece wrap of wing stroke

& woo   she warns me   both shes & me
    mater materiae wombs of black earth
or red earth or white earth or whatever-colored

-virgin-drift of transparent of sleeky river otter slick
     followed by diphthonged sacrificial English's
forty-four specific phonics

sounded out for her for us   star little fleeting we three
kissing crusts we three she-loaves
    baked close no matter what

     verge compounding convened & incorporate
before a tribunal of sachems counted as friends

& runaways/ adoptees/ hid attesters take me take us

before our connate comrades
beasts hankering
under the just auspices of here we are now

steamy   here-we-are-now Southern Sunday Jesus-proud
tar belt House of God
hotrods the local gunsmith tests his stock/ viral reports

he's buddies with the Troopers so nobody's complaining
but it's time for a cooling off
drop your firearm if you have   one a front's come in

so listen up trailer trash trophy buck twelve-point rack
canebrake rattlesnake skinned & tacked
to a varnished plywood plaque

listen up spanking bald bulb at the IGA listen up
roof rot plink plop   listen up incognito queen
of forgotten lost causes standing beside me

in the checkout line wisdom rises from the weirdest
places but don't ask/ sign's in the window
we don't accept no food stamps   around here

America freed her

             depending
   on your point   of view.

Konshattountzchette. Tall. Symmetrical.   Elegant.
Native. American. Indian. Mohawk. Depending.
You decide. Soldier of fortune.   Sachem of the 9th
Kentucky Infantry.   Favorite of Southern ladies.
Minié ball shivers his jaw
at Chickamauga.   Hideous aspect.   Beauty
spoilt:

   F l y i n g   C l o u d —

Appalachian. The Southern pronunciation is correct.   *Say:*
a-puh-LATCH-un. *Alleghenies.* Say: *AE-lə-gen-ez.*
North-central Pennsylvania to western Maryland
south to westernmost Virginia. Slaves openly
purchase tickets on the Allegheny Portage Railroad.
Escape Baltimore for Pittsburg. Baltimore's dozen
slave markets sell south for the cotton trade. Maryland
does not secede.   Never.   Secedes.

Delaware Creek Cherokee Seminole Kickapoo Seneca Osage
Shawnee Choctaw Lumbee Chickasaw Iroquois Powhatan
Pequot Ojibwa Huron Odawa Potawatomi Catawba
Pamunkey. All tribes fight with   *alongside*
assess the right   side.   Gain favor.

The Late Unpleasantness. The War of the Sections. The Brothers' War. War Between the States. War of the Rebellion. War for Southern Independence. War of Northern Aggression. Freedom War. War of Secession. Second American Revolution. War of Separation. War of

Calculation: Winner. Loser.

Relocate. Pacify. Reeducate. Remove.

America freed her

Monuments by Nature Require Brooding

Today. It's surreptitious shuttle. Back & forth across
the Mason Dixon Line. Today. It's domesticated.
Contained. *Almost*. This voluptuous verdurous callow
crippled country. This worst possible
shithole you can imagine. This trailer park trash these
fat cracker kids. Dollar Store Dollar General
Family Dollar.   *Yes.*

Yes ma'am. We have all the evidence you need
to despise us. Convictions viscous as dirt
daubers' nests   *Yes sir.* Stains
& seeds & worn out promises.
Pennants. Faded stars & bars. Old scars
never wed (the lone ranger took whatever she
could/ whatever came limping over the line
home).

Indisputable bona fides. Hand-to-hand combat
every every   *every single day*. Appomattox never
finished it off: monuments by nature require
brooding. Physically consistent metaphors. Hangers-on.
Stayers in the heat of. Daily encounters. Prodigals
intransigent. Foxholes in plain sight. The only story
we can ever. Reanimate with whatever

We still believe about *being*. That can't be
diminished can't be *taken back*. Role-play. Reenact
soldier. Householder. Even the most well-intentioned.
Can't begin to replicate.   Dress the part.
Don the uniform. Essential kit. Both sides' lice-infested.
Respect for the memory   of.   Proper exchange
of.   Casualties. Care for the wounded.

Today. We're tragi-comic spectators/ skirmish gawkers
history's witnesses lined up watching
behind an orange wattle plastic picket fence.

Sailor's Creek 1865 (Reenactment)

You   from the North or some other
country   you've entered
phantom land make-do kitchen
surgery   disembodied shins/ feet in a
mackerel barrel heap   severed
arms over there stiff hands
grasp air   — sullied
slab – the State Police ran tests:
it's real human blood.   You
every single one of you in this place this
day you want a spell to make you
him or her hiding biding
until carnage comes close enough
to home to flee to set off rifle pack slung
across your back baby draped in a shawl
at your breast I want you   *you*
captive delivered into each other's
territories camps shared cuts holes guts
the Chang & Eng of hill & hutch
clasp tight fix your ribcage bayonets
hearts beat wildly side by side   *you*
your bowels your balls your wombs
& ovaries your sons & daughters
classified white or brown or black to fight
or tend or serve or slave depending
on which side claims you.   You.   Perhaps
you're lazy or persistent truths
frighten you your children reigned-
in waiting for the tour guide to finish his
    speech. I want *you*
everybody here there then now
furloughed freed—
    desert for god's sake—

we're not cut out for what's
hobbling up the hill toward the Visitor's
Center a rebel yell *huzzah!* but *no* no hand-
to-hand-hewn fork staff sow shuffle
piedmont mire   instead
eight thousand ruined
            round soundless mouths

the iris the peony the dogwood bloom
(If War Comes to You)

Cerulean swarms the road burns the barns
exhausts everything in its path on the march in the fields
leaves the voided thumbnail scratch pod pulp behind   —

    the iris the peony the dogwood

White ooze is what we harvest now: furred orbs
sap seep silk crimson ragged flag blossoms twice
flowering first in present affliction & finally   —

    they're calling

Slit leech gum powder poppy pour palm lick suck
the clean the calm the holy battlefield balm banish all care plug
the arse up good on the move on hindsight's unfinished   —

    the iris the peony the dogwood   bloom

For argument's sake   or anecdote   or something
special: commemoration or celebration   or
frontline *ordinary*: dysentery amputation   —

    they're calling   for

Flesh &   *&* swallow & bone & fire roil up
to remind us where we stood then
where you stand   now.

               * * *

Shadow lifts his head   locks eyes with those
among us slipped between us   you'll never see   —
shimmery like white lies or good deeds gone nervy

    they're calling   *for rain*

Bad   he's in & out of focus bunked up
on an elbow stripped on a black sleeky
table laid edgeways/ head in hands he's skinned   —

    they're calling   *for rain*

He's muscled cartilaged mandibled a dumb-fuck
animal shivved & shucked
delivered.

    they're calling   *for*

               *   *   *

An oval framed photograph
turns its face to the wall for what comes
next is prescriptive:

    the iris the peony the dogwood   *bloom*

Lachrymal papaveris: God's nocturnal
tears; soldier's joy
before the bonesaw.

* * *

IV. *Grasp.*   *Unended.*

* * *

On June 30, 1908, a double ceremony took place in Buckingham, VA, when the corner stone was dedicated, and the shaft unveiled for the beautiful monument, the occasion bringing to that city the largest crowd that had ever assembled there. Veterans, Sons of Veterans, and the women whose part in the war had been so noble had gathered to do honor to the well-loved soldiers.

Confederate Veteran VOL. XVIII

Published by The Idylwood Studio, Scottsville, Va.
CONFEDERATE SOLDIERS' MONUMENT
BUCKINGHAM C. H., VA.
ERECTED BY THE LADIES OF BUCKINGHAM COUNTY. 1908

About Baltimore

Cross table slant bellow   sway verse reel
& span. Amidst the laird & bred & various
orthography morphology miscellany of empyrean
English. Starting in on. In on   *America*
the whole of it. Two chairs down dangling
the phrase drifts across/ around at dinner as though
the whole of it   *America* I mean   can be worked
out over coffee & pudding & the last of the good
Bordeaux. The whole of it. As dark & reckless
as godless in its manifold curses & distinctions
as all the indicted denizens of hell's cellar combined.

     The scald: Appalachian

For what's left of land when all the trees
get took. Scraped plain. When animals flee caves dens
lairs.   When birds flush & don't return.
Scalded   as in   *start over.*   Brace up. Reinforce. *About*

     Baltimore.

As if the whole damned city its mess & sordid
its mob & holy fucked-up its rectitude & whitewash
     cruel charm   its burned-out *might-of-beens*

Just murmurs. At table.   *About Baltimore.*   Scabbed.
Scarred over. Tore up. Healed. Scarred again. &
again. As riot. As march maybe. Or peacefully as in
rally. Or consummated like bought sex in cold
     wrath.   *Whatever.*   *Never mind.*

I close my eyes. Just for a moment. Polite. Politic. Change
the subject. Move on. Let it go. As if the whole as if the whole
        as if we   we I you everybody mutter
    stammer sum it up/ the terror shame grievance rage
by averting our eyes   *Baltimore* my Baltimore
      everybody's Baltimore   *going it blind.*

Baptist Dance

Living in thickness of dust   heap mounded
supine half-verbal obstructions. Blink. Startled
      at my own
greedy gorging human

voracity. Hours or days a month's
passing. Or no time at all. As mendacity is
      to the player/ veil to
lust.   I have plundered   I have staggered

I've sanded & primed & painted.
I have white surfaced
      smooth the bride her gown
in expectation. I have shore-lined braid-

stranded plains: libidinous sway   uncluttered
jealous in turn of nimbler prey. Moon to river
      rhythm to din
& ply   sleuth to shadow   dawn

to dance: *I loved you once* in a squall earworm
phrases turned continuous as echo sleeked my skin
      exactly the temperature
wet   of my skin. Unclothed & moving my hips

felt the same reported back explaining
why we come away in some ways changed
      embittered almost at the bliss
of chance   of luck   of passing by one

another: the night encounter.   Rival
the straightest route.
        Intercalations by moon or
sun stride or slumber   brood or mesmer.

I have lived in a village buried
in cinder stunned from the ruthless hacking
down of forests. Reliquaries carved in shapes
of birds & horses' heads have crowned me wild

boars ancient as any species ambled past
snuffling my palm; I'm enlisted I've earned
       their bristled persistence. I have won
the amulets   sloped   hand-scribed raw amber

clitorides (from the Greek *kleis:* a key
or latch) a hook.   I have swung rapt
the cat by its tail/ homologous penis: shaft to arrowhead
tongue-speaker-spoken   to revelation.

O Little Town (Listen)

O little town O little O little O magnified O my tiny
    town in the waking   the wake   Listen:

a heckling rooster my aurora river
    arise/ a rise amplified a body of water a boat's shanty
list/ parts of this canoe's construction I can't

control a sanctionless siege a breach
    lawless & ruleless velvet gold-thread-braided

epaulettes-in-charge Listen: O misanthropic leaker
    of misdeeds & feudal truths   Listen:
    O mystic O madman

O shaman of our own designs/ desires & if nothing else
    matters we're handy makers
    of tools & gadgets stakes & signs & homemade

munitions   Listen: Little Red Riding Hood's wolves
    caught in silver skim coat shivering
nibbling away at our ailments our noble failings pecking
    O bloodied

gob & comb at my shaky rudder/ tiller/ realm bob & cold white
embers dug in between my femur & fibula my tibia
my neurasthenic bone spurs & gristle Listen:
    the dull throb stabbing at alabaster

    with a screwdriver Listen: O hurricane strange

slide down a high high watery
      wall into a fathomless circumferentially small
pool slide down steep slippery steps
a holy spring a well   *am I siren or storm*   *caller*
    or called

into the sag O pious faultless upright O my little
Southern city of phantoms & shadows host
      of dread dreams & tribal illusions O Listen fleeting

O self-consumed sufferers O tired goblins of late-
      summer mercurochrome night of toxic antiseptic
outbreak/ our monuments' blather slinking over

      ever closer to our body's being/ fanning
eating away at our healthy tissues our moral
      parts asleep in respite

O wishing to wake months or years from now out of pain
    blameless   & healed

Claritas

stay the kept pair   leopard geckos tank-
trapped   & the bunnies
      this spring so brassy so emboldened grazing

the duskheap & stay cock's crow dewed sedge
crystalline shimmer & celestial claritas

    God in first light   & stay

our greatness & fineness & stay the one-trick
pony & its faulty idle rider & the current
candidates & single girls'

married girls' troubles & worries & the ice
storm brewing & stay rightwing radio rants &   &

    old-timey Calvinists the same

who live by the sword   die by the   & stay
the guy stockpiling off the internet an illegal

arsenal casting his own bullets for fun hiding
out in a Phoenix warehouse
    awaiting mob rule & the revolution &   & stay

the cab driver moved from Boston to St. Pete
his grievances   against the government
    & his ex-wife & stay

old weird America/ Matty Groves to Shady Grove
stay breathing space stay shiver & wrench six
circling above me

    waiting *watching* & stay
the ones describing voices of dread & doom
pledges & vows & stay breadcrumbs dropped

   to parse our politics/ stay
the hands that stroke the Liberty Bell
smoothing it soothing & patting as if
    as if it's a living

& stay reassurances & reminders that it's yet
needed   & stay Tiffany's Dream Garden

  one hundred thousand ground glass
squares curiously leached of color tools &
the muralist's mechanics of distancing

   the eye & suffering
the image & stay the first time I saw it sitting
on a bench a man's tongue in my mouth & stay

ravens fertile earth hauled away for a clean
   start new tract suburban basements

mined/ ripped open black by the block
six feet deep & stay
the disco I once frantic danced snorting
    Peruvian flake up my nose cut

with burning baby powder & stay
my America make me feel like a racist

regardless & stay this smoldering promised
land a span of joyed grief frenzied
   stretched out &
sweetening blithe & smiling fury

Green

> There wee landed and discouered a little way: but wee could find nothing worth the speaking of, but faire meddowes and goodly tall Trees; with such Fresh-waters running through the woods, as I was almost ravished at the first sight thereof.
> —George Percy, early Chesapeake Bay colonist

i.

        furthermore & in my solitude
after the first great growth comes the second great awakening
      & I alone fathom its secrets roughing it/ smoothing it

I alone bear speak/ ruse & shutter/ whim & cant that's human
parlance & illusion burnt taut   —leveled this roll-hitch plain set right
veteran peaks & bluffs—threadbare *Old Rag*   fierce *Hawksbill*

      mean *Poor*   I'll gather you Blue in my arms chafe cleft
& backbone make love love   *love to you* until I can't tell tilled
from my own pastel nose & my impolitic mouth reciting natural laws

& moral claims antiphons & countersuits to which in the background
       hum hum humming Powhatan Red Cloud Owen replies
we're still here we never left we're Chickahominy albeit our black bear

cougar & bobcat sleep in oblivion/ here here *here*   I'm graceless without
grace/ unbodied/ crude as lacking: see how I'm drawn surrounded stone
upon stone my peeling sills my rotting weatherboard: this frail palimpsest

ii.

Redneck cracker good old boy   accurate as anything I guess
Jack-pine savage too if you're looking north   just the same boys
are boys & a .22 is perfect for squirrel/ dead aim required/ sharpshooters
in homegrown wars   snipers in '67 trying hard not to die.

iii.

In meth lab country we shove rags in our mouths so nobody knows
we're abandoned.   Lately I hear more than I have in years.

iv.

If all my dreams came true I'd paint you big and let you—

v.

you molder you fodder you death's detail hovering in the field
where the goat shed stood or sitting on a stump in August
heat hot so hot nobody's paying attention scratching an itchy neck

reminding me how it works returned to places we knew
as us   bruise-less   unblemished   scars healed—
& if all my dreams came true I'd let you live & we'd ride side

by side & you'd ask me what's the name of that color & I'd swear
it's greenest green   & you'd argue *it's even greener
than that*   & it'd come to me then it's punch-drunk un-pruned

rub wound alive & don't die & tell the glory the rapture
the slaughter mess & wreckage & I'd repeat it over & over
as April turns to May & June unfolds & emerald glens

grow greener & swamps run thirsty in forest razor jade
& the years & decades & scores & centuries ain't hardly over   *no*
& the last splintered talk on our tongue's still fighting that war.

V. *Roughing it.*   *Smoothing it.*

* * *

Prester John's Book of Stars

i. Istrouma

>... and in savage [it is] called Istrouma which means red stick [bâton rouge], as at this place there is a post painted red that the savages have sunk there to mark the land line between the two [battling] nations...
>—André-Joseph Pénicaut, ca. 1723

        according to the expedition's indentured
woodworker carpenter half-honest storyteller the red
stick band resisted encroachment/ assimilation
    synchronicity/ red-painted war clubs
        or maybe they were

medicine wands we'll never know for certain
    the genesis people killed or captured & sold
in Saint Domingue   so

    there'll be no more stepping off that ledge
everyday no more self-policed
    torments & tortures no more nineteenth century Old
World empires bring on the revolutions roll
on new world order & the most recent toll this

    week by my count (but I've lost count count
count)   stands at ten

    & after the shafts hit their targets
a president pled unity: *a bullet need happen
    only once but for peace to work we need to
be reminded....*
        again & again &

again   a death ray not-quite-dartle too bright &
       the fire flash & echo
of a new-from-the-get-go clean slate   *or is it?*
      as the nation's sly grunt & beery
      dregs

as military madness hit-or-miss score-settling

    & retribution our cumulative consciences
wept drained   I've heard/ read white on black
white on white & black on black & no turning
back
    & Montrell in his blues tweets *please don't*

let please don't
let
please   *don't*

ii. Sunday, 17 July 2016

    These are trying times. Please don't let hate infect your heart.
    —tweeted on July 10, 2016, by Montrell Jackson, police officer killed
      on duty in Baton Rouge.

    a gleam of hope Montrell Montrell's
young forever thirty-one but his son will grow

up   I'm enough to crawl on my
knees & beg or jump this scarp way over
    to Sunday morning redemption our homegrown

    crucible/ what wondrous what wondrous
what
    to understand this alchemically-assigned
tragedy this place this time on earth
I'm afraid to say anything or nothing I'm white & unalterably

broken down there's a yellow line   *down*
    between us
    an American bison's maul a hermetic
museum to our antipathies/ blossomed rank &

    regiment I tote my lawn chair
down to the landing/ sip moonshine from a quart
        jar/ take cover/ elderly oak   ash   & walnut
from surge & torrent sure as hardwoods

    uprooted/ lifted upside-down in summer
storms/ driven straight-limbed grim-into-the-ground
        sure as every decade I've counted on this

    land sure as this river washes me/ us
clean/ blameless & that's that I'm past knowing color
past religion
        past clasped hands compacts past politics I live
        in the South for chrissakes Cradle of the
Confederacy I do know conflicted
equivocation/ insurgency standing both sides

of a line at once   sure as   as this river's
seen-everything-openly-under-the-sun sweat & eddy

iii. What Wondrous Love

> What wondrous love is this, O my soul, O my soul!
> What wondrous love is this, O my soul!
> What wondrous love is this that caused the Lord of bliss
> To bear the dreadful curse for my soul, for my soul,
> To bear the dreadful curse for my soul.
> —Appalachian Folk Hymn

    no fucked-up-ness fast enough to make up for
this payback/ reprisal/ this curse   a thaumaturge
is what we need

       a worker in wonders a performer
of miracles a frame an armature a means
by which to gather
       flank & furlough against wild-gunned fear fear
fears &
discharged ex-soldiers serving up red-eyed/ furious
matutinal horror shows salved by our black
& white & blue blood-salted maggot-filled
wounds   *please*

       we are all fellow travelers
       we are all fellow   travelers
       we are all   fellow

& in our awe & desperation readying to lose
limbs heads
hearts bellies & livers & lungs
on the day the poppies blossom   I call it

       stripped self-shackled/ unmanageable
right beside us all some say it will end when the flag
comes down some say when the guns are banned

              & gone

iv. Prester John

> ... Sundays were spoken of as the Paradises from the ravages of
> time (meaning that men literally didn't get any older on Sundays).
> —John Prest, *The Garden of Eden/The Botanic Garden and the
> Re-Creation of Paradise.* Yale University Press. 1981.

       & his legend of Ethiopian volunteers staring
for revelation down at coffee   grounds &
       cookie crumbs   what mourners say
coffin lids closed/ the heavens the divine

   set to lash rent in lamentation
   flay the unwary flesh

   the crime story of America or America's
Edenic aspirations & if we spoke as we
   walk
   sure of our direction full
of pursuit & insurrection as the earth

   & the four rivers of Paradise
   & the fertile crescent we learned

as children to touch the moon (that most female
   of heavenly orbs) & if our will goes
bonsai blunt is arousal our raison d'être
   arduous & exposed decaying &
murderous both at once *which is it?* stifled

life sure as *deal done* voluntarily
statutorily authorized & the Sunday dead

   never age or advance
while we dig holes until the sun
   breaks open & summer nights lure us spent
   of wine & water

Grinding Up the Seed Corn[3]

sacred as a name called aloud
in the night   a glandered horse a gasp
sighed/ turbulence so squally it shakes
the house the gap from crag to blunder   widening

wailing swell-tremored at once I'm withered
archive/ grim reflection honesty's deep
game played to waste all the seed corn
ground up & blown away

Parmelia colonies grasp branches & boulders
sheathed bed & curl   cuneiformed or antlered I speak
to them in voice of gravel clutch & cry
while tourists (red-rim-mouthed) lick their gelatos

* * *

snow's blown in now over our veranda
the woodpile's deep in knock & cover
brush filled up & bin smoke spiced lines a wind
wave hard beat north
          to south

my swamp laurel's budding   in December
gentle or rough   indifferent to please

* * *

---

3. An American Civil War-era phrase referring to the loss of a generation of young men.

walled cities emerge push out from cracked seed coats
& cotyledons miraculous chafe   or derelict
spectral tourists observe lapsed treaties wondering
what it must be like to lift such boulders
        mold mud bricks

I breathe familiar   appetent   I shove back
the pitch the black the hour cut cold through
nighttide's soft furred nap pods plume the chill
clear core polestars wink & squint
sainted/ sparkly in oxygen-less transmutation

in the bare bones house of was

> There's a song that will linger forever in our ears,
> Oh, hard times come again no more
> —Stephen Foster, "Hard Times Come Again No More," 1854

    wood smoke slur small hours stir
      telltale precipice   & terraced stretch

dearth & downpour drip from our tongues   our lips'
our thighs' hips' bellies' breasts'   superstitions

commonplace as serpent speak & safe our evening stars
this far north spilt skitter scape   our vapor blaze

our leaf litter bower/ rattle-clad panes
myopic mice/ long-whiskered/ scrape & tunnel bone-tired

we ache the day's tally
chores & obligations (half-asleep our sacked-out old
black cat)

tangent & impasse & argument spill
accord suspends & stumbles & right on schedule

our Pomegranate's made her first
      ruby bloom & by the hunter's light we think ourselves
untrammelled/ no more ties/ forgotten forsaken all

in our nakedness
but for their slipping in elbow to elbow side by silent
      side/ haint hind end & tailbone pressed
to bare wood boards   strange grammar soughs
    & sighs & stretches

backs to the wall a locust throb a hugger-muggle
this wattle hard house   *you*

       you move me so *so*

       we cannot will not leave you forgotten
abandoned & driven/ aggrieved as a fly-
       tormented cow
know us undaunted ready *ready*   in the day's last slant

       in slow burn hardwood in brittle-tinder pine
& poplar in red marl & James River mussels

we were every sort of fearless in our space & seasoned
       we were window box ruffle
paper rosy rose
       we were yellow daffodil-y we were open

every door   daring deluge risking bliss
       we were binge blooming   rain-chastened
hard times hard times come again come again   *no*

& Bless

        all the illness people all the streaming
pilgrims' barren scatter stripling bark
& tender & bless the bandit's head
        rolling/ stalling
staring/ moth to moon dusk
to cavern ebon nail gnawed
&   stub
      &   yes god bless   god *bless*
this packed plaza today's & yesterday's suns'
deep reserve glint &
fracture a fallen woman's foreign veil
& stoned her kin deny her/ prostrate
for her life for living/ being & bless
the skittered lifeblood under
the floorboards between

plates & piers gallanting out bold
before dawn its supine back-wriggle
striped comings & goings & bless
the rift-open aura
illumined astral pink morning watercolor
wash along the blue ridge I stammer
as a child my attachments to objects
misunderstood as linkage as hairy-
stalked kudzu climbs the boxwoods'
backs; lovers or foes?
      & bless the bumbling bamboo
too ruinous   &

every spring's speckless ripped
blade & bucket   & bless   &
    bless *bless* the kleptomaniacal
    ruling class's

Panglossian sputter pompous
lapse & unbelieving slumber I bless
this copse this gussied-up graveside chat
antipodal woolly muddied
smear what drear measure
    what a month to die

& bless our slave chapel moved
over harrowed field & passion smoothed
over hanks & marrow
    hees & yaws & wept white
amplitude scale & hands that
blind & feed some bone
    some splint some salt
glazed sherd a shine plucked
clean from rubble   silica & sodium
vapor dure: the potter's thumb prints
    fired forever in wet smoke & rouged

iron oxide & bless the hangers-
    on released to creep &
tarry matched sets paired birds all set

for the Sunday   shoot & bless the frog-
of-the-field stacked bump-backed
& clutching one atop another in a bucket
on the feeding floor
     & bless this breeding wire
this hedged tendril   &
foothold tension rib & shore
     & bless the suffocate ivy
clutch & ramble cling-stem stout
roof pitch &
     stroke & bless & *bless*
the survivors   today's &
     yesterday's & yes *yes* bless
all these crumbling castes

* * *

You have to bend double to find them, peering up through the forest of brown canes and pale green shoots and yellowing leaves to where they dangle, protected from wind and sun, on filaments almost too fine to bear their weight. They hang in jeweled clusters purple in the shade, translucent crimson where a sunbeam catches them.
—Samuel Chamberlain, *Fair is Our Land*,
Hastings House, 1946

* * *

Notes

The images in this manuscript were sourced from documents in the Walter Lloyd Fontaine Papers collection in the archives of the Virginia Museum of History & Culture, Richmond, Virginia. Walter Lloyd Fontaine lived from 1786 until 1860 and was the original owner of the author's farmhouse and the land on which it still stands. Three exceptions include the print on page 53, entitled *Top of the Blue Ridge, 1954*, by Carson Davenport; on page 2 the anonymous photograph of the author's home in New Canton, Buckingham County, Virginia, and on page 66 the author's photograph of one of its post & beam corner braces. All images are reproduced with permissions.

Acknowledgments

How to Make a Place in the World, Mara Adamitz Scrupe, solo
    exhibition catalogue, Indiana State University Press, 2010:
Flood Stage
Wolf Trees

Aesthetica Creative Writing Award in Poetry Anthology, prize
    finalist, UK 2015:
Groundhog Laws of Contiguity

Axon Journal, University of Canberra, Australia, Summer 2018:
Surrender Not Peace/ Young Man Standing beside Empty Chair
with Kepi and Worn Boots, ca. 1865
& Other Things Besides

Narrative Magazine Editors Prize, finalist, web publication, 2016:
Wanderer
Prester John's Book of Stars

Ruminate Magazine 2015 Janet B. McCabe Poetry Prize Anthology,
    finalist:
the iris the peony the dogwood bloom (If War Comes to You)

Canterbury Poetry Festival/ University of Kent Prize and Poet of the
    Year Anthology, short listed, UK 2015:
Baptist Dance

Narrative Magazine, Winter 2015:
Sailors Creek 1865 (Reenactment)
Plantation as Idyll

Hedgehog Press Anthology, *Other People's Freedoms*, Fall 2018:
Monuments by Nature Require Brooding

Crab Creek Review, Summer 2016:
Grinding Up the Seed Corn

Cornwall Poetry Festival Competition Anthology, winners and short listed poems anthology, UK 2016:
Claritas

University of Canberra Vice-Chancellor's Poetry Award Anthology, short listed, Australia 2015:
About Baltimore

Sentinel Literary Quarterly Poetry Competition, Third Prize, December 2016:
& Bless

MARA ADAMITZ SCRUPE is a visual artist, a poet, and the author of six award-winning poetry collections. Her fellowships include NEA CEC/ArtsLink, Washington, DC Arts Commission, Virginia Museum of Fine Arts, Virginia Arts Commission, MacDowell Colony, Djerassi Foundation, Tyrone Guthrie Centre/Ireland, Montalvo Arts Center, Irish Museum of Modern Art Artist Fellowship Programme, and USF Verftet-AiR/Bergen. Her poems have been published widely in national and international literary magazines, journals, and anthologies, and she has won or been shortlisted for Canterbury International Arts Festival Poet of the Year (UK), Brighthorse Poetry Book Prize (USA), Grindstone International Poetry Competition (UK), Fish Prize (Ireland), Aesthetica Award (UK), Erbacce-press Poetry Book Prize (UK), Plough Prize (UK), Ron Pretty Prize (Australia), Cornwall Festival Competition (UK), Canberra Vice-Chancellor's Award, (Australia), and National Poetry Competition (UK), among others. Mara is a marathon runner, an accordionist, and art professor and dean of the School of Art, University of the Arts, Philadelphia, USA. She lives with her husband on their farm overlooking the James River in central Virginia.